PEASANT FOODS
KIDS CAN MAKE AT HOME

JJ CARROL

First Published in the United States by Jackson Marbles, an imprint of Quality Business Communications, Inc., Birdsboro, Pennsylvania, USA. 2023.

Copyright © 2023 by JJ Carroll.
Cover image: Reproduction by Gholamreza Shoghmand Nazarloo: Public domain image from German cookbook, Kuchenmaistrey, 1485

Internal tracings and photographs by JJ Carroll.

All rights reserved. No part of this publication may be reproduced, stored or transmitted in any form or by any means, electronic, mechanical, photocopying, recording, scanning, or otherwise without written consent permission from the publisher. It is illegal to copy this book, post it to a website, or distribute it by any other means without permission. Write to **info@qubcomm.com.**

This book is for families and middle school aged youth education groups. It is intended to replicate an age-appropriate dining experience, not a cooking experience.

Recipes are tested in our kitchen and modified as needed with modern ingredients and cooking techniques.

Some recipes are simple while others use a hot stove or oven, or sharp objects such as knives or cheese grater. Adults should supervise students or assist accordingly.

Kids can also enjoy the coloring pages, puzzles and other activities they'll find throughout the book.

Recipes

Breakfast
Peasant Bread 7
Bread Starter 8
Homemade Butter 10
Goat Cheese/Cream Cheese 11

Main Meal
Vegetable Broth 13
Pottage 14
Peas Pottage 15
Salmon with Sorrel 15

Beverages
Ginger Ale 19
Root Beer 20
Apple Cider 21

Supper
Soft Boiled Eggs 23
Hard Boiled Eggs 23
Pickled Eggs 23
Porridge 24
Oatcakes 26

Treats
Honey and Goat Cheese 28
Berries and Cream 28
Gingerbrede 29
Barley Pudding 30
Custard Pie 31

Coloring Page:

Introduction

The Middle Ages spanned an entire millenium from the late 5th to the late 15th centuries. That's a long time to think that nothing would have changed. Politics, ecomony and other factors had plenty of time to impact the population's diet in different parts of the world.

In fact, when we think of Medieval times, many of us think of Europe. But which part of Europe comes to your mind? England? France? Germany? Spain? Each of these places had different foods available to peasants based on climate, soil, trade routes and more. They may even have different definitions of the term "peasant."

For this peasant foods cookbook, we took a very general view. Most of these recipes can be modified according to whatever grows in a specific area of study. Have fun mixing them up and making your own recipes!

Research challenge

Label the countries and color code them by primary grain grown in each country.

Breakfast

Breakfast wasn't a typical meal until the later Middle Ages. It started as an extra meal for the sick, but then helped give morning strength to peasants before they went to work in the fields. Bread and butter was considered a countryman's breakfast. They may also have had a hunk of cheese or leftovers from the previous night's supper.

Coloring Page: (public domain image)

Peasant Bread

Peasants ate a lot of bread. It was the main part of their diet. This recipe is easy for kids to make because you don't have to *knead* the dough. Just whisk everything together. Of course, it's still bread so it does take a little bit of patience to let it rise. That's a process where air bubbles form to make it fluffy. Because the dough pours easily, you can use any shaped pan to make this bread.

Ingredients:

- 4 cups flour (you can use all-purpose or whole wheat for this recipe)
- 1 ½ teaspoons salt
- 2 teaspoons sugar
- 1 packet active dry yeast
- 2 cups warm water

Medieval cooks used a glob of bread starter instead of yeast to make their bread rise.

See next page to learn more.

Instructions:

Step 1. Mix the flour, salt, sugar and yeast in a large bowl.

Step 2. Add the warm water to the dry ingredients. Stir and scrape sides until all dry ingredients are blended.

Step 3. Cover the bowl of dough with a cloth let rise about 90 minutes. The finished dough will be sticky.

Step 4. Preheat oven to 425°. Use a pan spray or butter to grease a bread pan or baking dish. Scrape bowl to pour the dough directly into the pan.

Step 5. Let the dough rest in pan 20 minutes.

Step 6. Bake 15 minutes. Reduce to 375° and bake additional 20 minutes. Remove from oven and let it cool.

Bread Starter

Medieval cooks didn't have dry yeast like we have today. Instead, they used a fermented bread dough, or sourdough starter. A good cook would have a crock of bread starter ready to go because they used it every day.

If necessary, cooks can develop a new (or replenish a lost) batch of bread starter with ingredients they had on hand. All it takes is flour and water – and time.

Bacteria is the third ingredient but you don't have to buy it. The good bacteria that is in the air will find its way to your bread starter. Bacteria can taste different from place to place. That's why when you travel, bread never tastes quite like it does at home.

Here's how you can make, feed and use your own jar of sourdough starter.

Notes:

- Bread starter can take 1 to 2 weeks to become "active." So plan ahead.
- Always use lukewarm water.
- Whole wheat flour works best to get it started. You can switch over to white flour on the third day. (You can also try other flours, such as rye.)
- The starter develops best when kept at room temperature (about 69° to 72° F or 21° to 22° C). Colder storage can slow or prevent fermentation.

Source: Modified from King Arthur Bread Company at: www.kingarthurbaking.com/recipes/sourdough-starter-recipe

Bread Starter cont...

Ingredients:

- Flour (Any kind of bread flour will work: all-purpose, whole wheat, rye, etc. If you have it, start with whole wheat Days 1 and 2 before switching to all-pupose.)
- Water
- Clean, clear quart-size mason or other jar with lid

Instructions:

Day 1: Mix ½ cup each of flour and warm water in the jar. Make sure the flour is completely mixed in with the water. Place the jar somewhere at room-temperature for 24 hours.

Day 2: Remove half of the mixture and throw it away or add to a bread or cake recipe. You should have ½ cup of mixture left. Add another ½ cup water and 1 cup flour. Mix thoroughly, replace the lid and let sit another 24 hours.

Day 3: You should start to see bubbles form. Keep only ½ cup of mixture (use or throw the rest away). Then add ½ cup water and 1 cup flour. Mix thoroughly, replace the lid and return to storage.

Days 4 - 7: Create a twice daily (every 12 hours) routine of keeping ½ cup of previous mixture, and adding ½ cup water and 1 cup flour. Each day should bring more bubbles and activity. It should be wet and oozy, smell fruity and grow to 2 ½ cups or higher. See picture on previous page.

Days 8+: You should have a living bread starter by Day 7. If not, try a warmer storage or keep feeding it another few days until it looks and smells right.

To use in bread recipes in place of yeast:

For a single loaf of bread, you'll need about 1 cup of ripe sourdough starter stirred down. This will add moisture to your dough, so adjust other liquid in your recipe as needed. Dough made with starter may take 4 to 24 hours to rise, so test it and plan ahead if making bread for a special occasion.

Continue to feed remaining starter, or store in refrigerator up to 10 days. Wake it up with feedings about 2 to 3 days before use.

Homemade Butter

Need butter for your peasant bread? Here's a great project for kids.

Ingredients:

- 8 ounces heavy whipping cream
- 1/8 teaspoon salt
- 1 clean, dry quart-sized mason jar
- 2 or 3 clean, dry marbles
  (optional: marbles help to speed up the process, but are not required.)

Kids can take turns passing the jar around. It can take up to 15 minutes, depending on how strong you are and how hard you shake.

Instructions:

It's easy! Do it to music with an awesome fast beat and it will be fun, too.

Step 1: Pour the heavy cream into a mason jar, add marbles, secure the lid and shake, shake, shake! (Shake the jar, not yourself.)

Step 2: Keep shaking the jar until you can't hear the marbles anymore.

Step 3: Open the jar and peer inside. It probably looks like whipped cream. That's because it IS now whipped cream! It's time to add a pinch of salt and shake, shake, shake some more.

Step 4: Listen for clunking inside the jar. It should form a soft solid with the buttermilk separated.

Goat Cheese or Cream Cheese

Peasants ate "green cheese," which doesn't mean it was green. It means it wasn't aged like other cheeses. Depending on the source of your milk, this recipe can make goat cheese (from goat's milk) or cream cheese (from cow's milk).

Equipment:

- Medium saucepan
- Long-handled stirring spoon
- Colander
- Deep bowl
- Cheesecloth
- Cooking thermometer

Ingredients

- 1 quart whole milk or goat's milk.
- 3 tablespoons of an acid source such as lemon juice or vinegar. This will impact the flavor so choose based on your tastes. (Clear distilled vinegar is the most neutral.)
- Salt (optional)

Instructions:

Step 1: Heat milk in the pot. When it reaches 180° F, remove from heat.

Step 2: Stir in the lemon juice or vinegar. Watch it for about 15 seconds. The milk should start to form chunks. If not, stir in a little more vinegar or juice.

Step 3: Line your colandar with several layers of cheesecloth. Gently pour (or spoon) in your solids to drain off the liquids.

Step 4: Gather up the 4 corners of the cheesecloth and tie together so the cheese is inside a packet. Hang the packet from a long spoon handle and set over a deep bowl so it can drain until it is a thick cottage cheese texture.

Step 5: If desired, transfer to a bowl and stir salt or herbs into the soft cheese. Then mold or press the cheese into a ball, tube or hockey puck shape. Store in the refrigerator and use within one week.

Main Meal

There was no such meal called "lunch," but "dinner" was served anywhere between 10 a.m. and 2 p.m. Dinner was the heartiest meal of the day. For peasants, that included more bread and butter, plus whatever they grew in their personal gardens. They rarely ate meat because it was expensive. Anything that ran in the forests would have belonged to the land owners. Sometimes they had fish if they lived near a river.

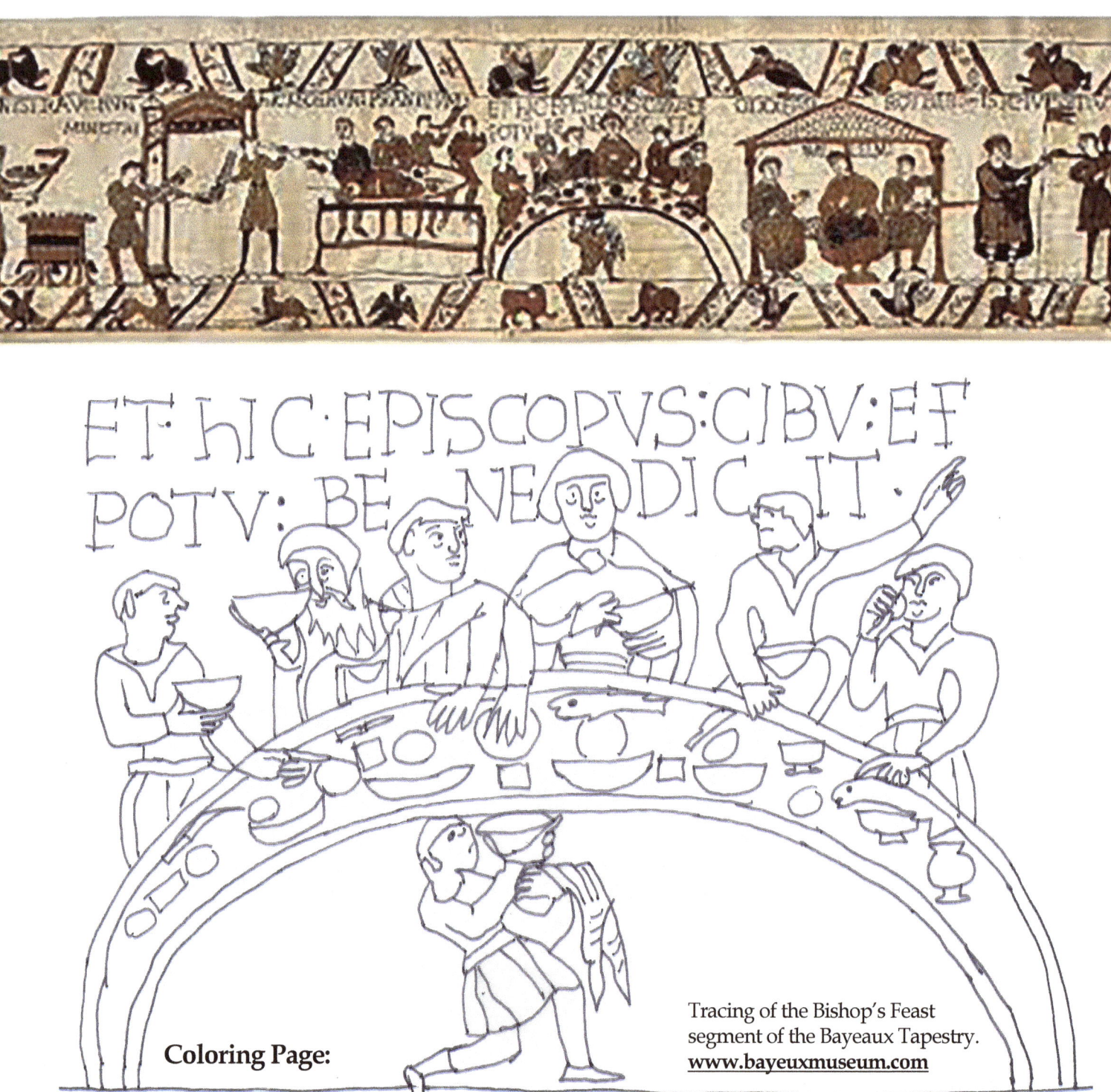

Coloring Page:

Tracing of the Bishop's Feast segment of the Bayeaux Tapestry.
www.bayeuxmuseum.com

Vegetable Broth

Boil vegetables in water and you'll get cooked vegetable. Let them boil long enough to flavorize and color the water, and you'll have a nutritious liquid called pot liquor or broth. You can drink it or use it in recipes.

Ingredients:

- 2 carrots
- 2 stalks celery
- 1 medium onion
- 6 to 10 cloves garlic (to your taste)
- 1 bunch parsley
- 6 sprigs thyme
- 2 large bay leaves
- 2 quarts water

Add any of these (if you want):
2 medium turnips
1 bunch spring onions
2 leeks
2 tomatoes*
Salt

Instructions:

Step 1: Cut the vegetables to about 1-inch cubes and add to the pot.

Step 2: Heat oil in the pot and add the vegetables and herbs. Cook until soft and brown.

Step 3: Add water. Cook on high until boiling, then reduce heat. Cover the pot to prevent evaporation. Cook at least 30 minutes.

Step 4: Taste test the broth and cook longer if needed.

Step 5: Strain out the mushy vegetables and throw them in the garden.

You now have a flavorful broth to help make your pottage soup taste better than if you just use water. See next page for details.

*Tomatoes are a great way to add flavor, color and nutrition to your broth. However, Tomatoes were not widely cultivated in Europe until the 18th century so would not be part of an authentic Medieval broth recipe.

Pottage

Pottage was a mainstay food for peasants. It could be a soup or a stew depending on how much broth, vegetables and grain you use. You can make it with water, but it will taste better with broth. You can also mix up the vegetables and use the ones you like best. You cook it to fit your taste. There's no right or wrong way. (See image page 16.)

Ingredients:

Start with:	Add any of these as desired:	Season with:
2 quarts broth	1 head cabbage, chopped	1 bay leaf
2 stalks celery	2 whole leeks, chopped	½ teaspoon thyme
2 carrots	2 medium turnips	½ teaspoon rosemary
1 medium onion	1 cup peas or beans	1 teaspoon parsley
2 cloves garlic	½ cup rice or barley	Salt and pepper (optional)

Instructions:

Step 1: Cut up the vegetables you choose to use.

Step 2: Put a splash of broth in your cooking pot and cook vegetables until tender and starting to brown.

Step 3: Add herbs and remaining broth. Bring everything to a boil.

Step 4: Reduce heat and simmer at least 15 min or until vegetables, beans and grains are soft.

Add more to make it thicker.

More veggies will make it heartier. More grains will make it thicker.

Potatoes and tomatoes were not yet introduced in Europe during the middle Ages. But you can add with other vegetables if you wish. A cup of leftover mashed potatoes is also a great way to thicken your soup.

Peas Pottage

Peas are nutritious as well as filling. Also called "peas porridge," they were probably served mushier than you're used to.

Ingredients:

- 1 cup fresh peas
- 1 cup vegetable broth
- A sprig of sage, parsley, or mint

Instructions:

Step 1: Put all ingredients in a small pot and bring to a boil. Reduce heat to medium and simmer 45 minutes.

Step 2: Mash the soft peas.

Salmon and sorrel

If a family lived near a river and had permission to fish in it, then salmon might have been a frequent dish at their table. For this recipe, you'll use a mortar and pestle to grind sorrel leaves to release their juices. If you can't find sorrel in your grocery store, try another tart flavor source such as rhubarb.

Ingredients:

- Butter (1 tablespoon per 2 pieces of fish)
- A 1-inch-thick piece of salmon per person (bring to room temperature before cooking)
- Salt and pepper (optional)
- 4 leaves of sorrel per serving

Instructions:

Step 1: Melt butter over medium heat. Salt and pepper the salmon, as desired.

Step 2: Place the salmon pieces in the pan to fry about 3 - 4 minutes per side.

Step 3: While salmon is cooking, crush the sorrel leaves in the mortar.

Step 4: Wrap the crushed leaves in cheese-cloth and squeeze juice over the fish.

Did you know...

Before plates, bowls and flatware were common, people used their bread, called a trencher, to hold their food. See page 7 for bread recipe. If you use a pie dish to shape your dough, you can slice off the top of the finished bread and put your food on the plate-shaped bottom part. Or scoop out the inside of a bowl-shaped bread and add your pottage. Tear up remaining bread to scoop up your food or sop up liquids.

Common Medieval Ingredients
Word Search Puzzle

```
R S D S B R E A D S T A R T E R L N N C L
O B W F E H A X D G H G H D B O D R A T T
L M C J P E P K D T R P S V I M I B N D A
L U S V A A R J V D M E A E F G B C X U J
E R U P R V I T Q C E A E K L A K C F W O
D C S S Y C U T W K R Q N G P F L O U R
O D N K L C O F R I B S J E B L P X L P S
A A O B E R T N O M U P V I N E G A R S K
T E Y P Y E S R S E I R R E B W A R T S H
S R R Q K A L Z E A A U F U Q Z B N I W Y
Y B V P T M Z L M W W Q Z E L Y E G S T K
C H I C K E N S A N D E G G S E T C X L B
U G F Q P C Q P R M E L O N S N L H I A A
R C Z A I D B L Y C K U G C X O M M Y S R
R W A L N U T S R Y U C S Y V H S T I M L
A C C R K J W O S A F X O E E T W U L C E
N T O O R R E G N I G W S O A D K R S S Y
T E T S N O B D I I N E A O X J T N L V F
S S U Q M C T N A Q O L G W V K M I Q H G
F A E L Y A B S R S M N H K J K I P W W N
D R H N U A X S G S F O S E C Y X S S B U
```

Apples	Chicken and eggs	Green Beans	Rolled Oats
Apricots	Cloves	Heavy Cream	Rosemary
Barley	Currants	Honey	Salt
Bay Leaf	Flour	Leeks	Strawberries
Bread crumbs	Fruit Trees	Melons	Thyme
Bread Starter	Gingerroot	Onions	Turnips
Cabbage	Goats Milk	Parsley	Vinegar
Carrots	Grains	Pears	Walnuts

Beverages

Many believed that Medieval people drank a lot of ale (beer) because the water was poluted. Researches now know that's not true, at least not everywhere. But beer was more robust and nutritious than water and so they drank it.

Here you'll find kid-friendly ale and cider recipes to serve at home.

Coloring Page: Tracing of Monk Tasting Wine From a Barrell. From Li Livres dou Santé by en: Aldobrandino of Siena. (Public Domain)

Ginger Ale Syrup

Ingredients:

- 4 ounces fresh ginger root, cut into ¼ inch slices
- 1½ cups water
- ½ cup sugar
- ½ cup honey
- 1/8 teaspoon salt
- Juice of 2 limes

To make ginger ale from syrup:

Mix ¼ cup ginger syrup with a glass of club soda.

Source: Americaskitchen.com. Ginger Ale. Available at: www.americastestkitchen.com/kids/recipes/ginger-ale. Accessed September 5, 2022.

Instructions:

Step 1: In medium saucepan, combine sliced ginger, water, sugar, honey, and salt. Bring to simmer over medium heat (small bubbles should break often across surface of mixture).

Step 2: Reduce heat to medium-low and cook, stirring occasionally with wooden spoon, for 15 minutes. Turn off heat and slide saucepan to cool burner.

Step 3: Stir in lime juice. Let mixture cool completely, about 30 minutes.

Step 4: Strain the mixture through cheesecloth. Press gently on ginger pieces to extract as much liquid as possible. Pour strained ginger syrup into jar with tight-fitting lid. Refrigerate up to 1 week.

Quicker-n-easier Ginger Ale

If you don't mind pulp in your orange juice, then maybe you won't mind it in your ginger ale either.

Ingredients:

- Ginger root
- Juice of 1/2 lime
- Club soda

Instructions:

Step 1: Grate 1 teaspoon of ginger into a tall glass.
Step 2: Squeeze the lime juice over it.
Step 3: Add ice and fill glass with club soda.

Root Beer Syrup

Ingredients:

- ½ oz dried burdock root (cut into thick slices)
- 1 teaspoon dried whole coriander seeds
- 1 whole star anise
- 1 whole clove
- 6 cups water
- ¼ cup dark molasses, not blackstrap
- 3 teaspoons sassafras extract*
- 1/8 teaspoon wintergreen extract
- Up to 6 cups sugar

Instructions:

Step 1: Place all the spices (burdock, coriander, anise, and clove) in a large saucepan that has a tight-fitting lid. Pour in the water and bring to a boil over high heat. Drop the heat to low, cover and simmer for 15 minutes.

Step 2: Add the molasses, stir, replace the lid, and return to a simmer for 5 minutes.

Step 3: Remove the pan from the heat, stir in the wintergreen and sassafras extracts, replace the lid and let the mixture cool.

Step 4: Strain the liquid through cheesecloth.

Step 5: Measure the strained liquid. Return it to the rinsed pot and add an equal amount of sugar, by volume, to the pot.

Step 6: Bring the mixture to a boil, drop the heat to low and let simmer for 5 minutes.

Step 7: Pour the syrup into jars and store in the refrigerator up to a year.

To make root beer from syrup:

Stir in 1 to 3 tablespoon of syrup (to your taste) per cup of club soda.

Source: Adapted from: "Steve" Recipes.net. Root Beer Extract Recipe (A&W Copycat). Available at: https://recipes.net/side-dish/dip-sauces/root-beer-extract-recipe-aw-copycat/. Accessed September 5, 2022.

*Original recipe called for 3 oz dried sassafras root but that proved difficult to find. I adapted the recipe to use extract instead.

Apple Cider

You can mix and match apples as you like. Adjust the sugar based on if your apples are sweet or tart. I used sweet Honeycrisp apples, so I didn't need as much sugar.

Equipment

- Large stock pot (with or without strainer)
- Cheesecloth

Ingredients:

- 10 large apples (about 5 ½ pounds) washed and cut into quarters. No need to peel or core.
- 5 quarts plus 1 cup hot water
- ¾ cups sugar (less if desired or using sweet apples)
- 1 tablespoon cinnamon
- 1 tablespoon allspice

Instructions:

Step 1: Add all ingredients to the pot. Turn burner on high to bring to boil.

Step 2: Reduce heat to medium and gently boil uncovered for 1 hour.

Step 3: Reduce heat to low, cover, and simmer for 2 hours.

Step 4: Remove apple pulp from the liquid and set aside.

Step 5: Line colander with 3 layers of cheesecloth. Place colander in a large bowl. Add apple pulp and press to squeeze out remaining liquid.

Step 6: Add squeezed pulp liquid to original strained liquid. Stir to blend.

Step 7: Strain blended liquid one more time using fresh cheesecloth.

Step 8: Pour cider into pitcher and chill for four hours.

Supper

Supper was not the main meal of the day, but rather a light end to a hard day's work. A family probably ate more bread or perhaps a cereal in the form of a hot bowl of grain or baked into a cookie or flat cake. They may have had eggs and more cheese. If there were leftovers from dinner, then supper might have been a bigger affair.

Coloring Page: Tracing of After the Harvest by Peiter Aertsen. (Public Domain)

Eggs

Eggs were an inexpensive and, therefore, popular food with peasants. They were forbidden during certain religeous times like Lent, but otherwise a grateful and nourishing addition to the peasant diet.

Soft Boiled

Step 1: Fill a medium pot with water and bring it to boil over high heat. Gently add eggs, one at a time with a spoon. Do not let them drop.

Step 2: Boil for 4 minutes.

Step 3: Scoop each egg out with the spoon. Transfer hot eggs to a bowl of ice water and let them cool enough to handle. Carefully peel the eggs and serve warm.

Hard Boiled

Step 1: Gently place raw eggs in medium pot. Fill with enough cold water to cover the eggs. Place on burner set to high heat. Bing to boil.

Step 2: Reduce heat to medium and gently boil for 15 minutes.

Step 3: Transfer hot eggs to a bowl of ice water and let them cool. Serve cold.

Pickled

Ingredients:

- 3 cups white vinegar
- 1 cup water
- 1 teaspoon coarse salt
- 1 large onion (thinly sliced)
- 1 bay leaf
- 1/3 cup sugar
- 1 dozen hard boiled eggs, peeled

Instructions:

Step 1: Add everything except eggs to the pot. Turn burner on high to bring to boil.

Step 2: Reduce heat and simmer for 5 minutes.

Step 3: Put the eggs in a large jar and pour hot liquid over them. Allow to cool.

Step 4: Refrigerate at least 7 days.

Porridge

Porridge is an old term used for boiled grain. It can have different names based on the grain used. If you use oats, you probably call it oatmeal. If you use buckwheat, you might call it kasha.

Oat porridge was a popular breakfast in medieval Scotland. That's because oats grew easily on the rough Scottish hillsides.

Whole oats from medieval times took a long time to cook. Some people soaked them overnight to speed up the cook time. This recipe uses "rolled" oats or "old-fashioned" oats. That means the oat was steamed and rolled into flakes.

If you buy "instant" oats, then follow the package directions. Instant oats are also rolled, but they're cut thinner and will cook faster.

Porridge cont...

Ingredients:

1 Serving:
- ½ cup rolled oats
- 1 cup water

2 Serving:
- 1 cup rolled oats
- 1 ¾ cup water

4 Serving:
- 2 cup rolled oats
- 3 cup water

Instructions:

Step 1: Bring water to boil on high heat.

Step 2: Add oats and stir.

Step 3: Immediately turn down the heat to simmer. Watch the cook pot so it doesn't boil over. Stir if necessary until it calms down.

Step 4: Set a timer for 6 minutes (or according to package instructions). When all the liquid has soaked into the oats, your oat porridge (oatmeal) is done.

Change it!

Try broth instead of water. You can also use milk or a combination of milk and water. If you use milk, do not bring to full boil and stir often to prevent scalding.

Fix it!

- **Undercooked?** Add more liquid and cook covered to help it soak in.
- **Too watery?** Cook uncovered a little longer to evaporate the excess liquid.
- **Too thick or pasty?** Stir in a bit of milk.

Top it!

Use these suggestions or make up your own!

- Salt and butter were common toppings in old times.
- Sweeten it naturally with what peasants had on hand like berries.
- Drizzle it with honey or maple syrup.

Oatcakes

Depending on the century and country, peasant food was often for survival, not entertainment. These oatcakes may look like our familiar oatmeal cookies, but they're missing a lot of yummy ingredients that many peasants couldn't get easily. Yet, they were simple to make and served their purpose in nutrition.

You can also roll out the dough and use a small round cookie cutter or large round hamburger press for a flatter result, like a rice cake (with similar taste.)

Ghee them up with butter, jam, cheese or honey.

Ingredients:

- 2¼ cup oats
- 1/3 cup flour
- 1 teaspoon salt
- ½ teaspoon baking soda
- 1 tablespoon honey
- 4 tablespoons softened butter
- 1/3 cup boiling water

Instructions:

Step 1: Preheat oven to 350°. Mix together the oats, flour, salt, baking soda and honey. Add the butter and rub together until all mixed in large crumbles.

Step 2: Gradually pour in hot water and mix to form a thick, sticky dough.

Step 3: Use ice cream scoop to drop onto baking tray. OR: Roll out on floured board to a half inch thick. Cut small or large round shapes to place on baking sheet.

Step 4: Bake 20 mins or until golden.

Treats

Dessert wasn't really a thing in Medieval times, but they may have had a treat now and then or during special feasts. Peasants generally satisfied their sweet tooth and enhanced their recipes with nature's candy like fresh fruits, melons, berries and honey.

In later Medieval years, sugar and exotic spices like cinnamon became available but it was expensive. Still, I have included a few recipes that call for these less-likely ingredients.

Honey and Goat Cheese

Swirl some honey into your goat cheese and spread it on bread or crackers. It's simply delicious!

Berries and Cream

Ingredients:

- 2 cups sliced strawberries
- 1/4 cup sugar
- 1/4 cup heavy cream (un-whipped)

Ingredients:

Step 1: Mix berries and sugar gently in a bowl.

Step 2: Let stand for 30 minutes.

Step 3: Spoon into serving dishes.

Step 4: Drizzle with cream.

Gyngerbrede
(Gingerbread)

The gyngerbrede that Geoffrey Chaucer and William Shakespeare wrote about was nothing like the gingerbread we shape into little men or walls of a house.

Medieval gingerbread was a moist bar with a consistency closer to that of a brownie. Ginger is a spice with a bite. Adding honey to it made it a candied treat.

Source: Recipe modified from
https://onlinemuseum.net/cuisine/gingerbread/medieval-gingerbread

Ingredients:
- 1 cup honey
- ½ cup breadcrumbs
- 2 teaspoon ground ginger
- ½ teaspoon pepper

Ginger is a natural remedy for settling an upset stomach. That makes it the perfect end to a hearty meal.

Instructions:

Step 1: Boil honey and skim off the layer of foam. This was called "clarifying" the honey in Medieval times.

Step 2: Turn heat down and stir in breadcrumbs and spices.

Step 3: Press the mixture into a baking tin and leave to cool.

Step 4: Once cooled, cut it into squares (about 1 ½ inches).

Barley Pudding

This treat is similar in flavor and texture to rice pudding, but more common in areas that grew barley instead.

Ingredients:

- 1 cup pearled barley
- 4 ½ cups water
- ½ teaspoon salt
- ½ cup raisins*
- 1/3 cup sugar
- 1/3 cup heavy cream

*Instead of raisins, try currents or dried and chopped apricots or apples.

Or toss in a handful of fresh berries as shown.

Instructions:

Step 1: Add barley, and water to medium pot. Bring to boil. Reduce heat and simmer for 40 minutes. (Add 20 minutes if you use whole barley instead of pearled.)

Step 2: Add the raisins (or dried fruit) and simmer for another 15 minutes, until the barley is soft.

Step 3: Stir in the sugar and cream. Let stand about 15 minutes to cool and thicken. Serve warm.

Source: Modified from: www.daringgourmet.com/scottish-barley-pudding/

Custard Pie

Those who had access to sugar and spices could enjoy this yummy treat. See how the cinnamon rises to the top for a delicious burst of flavor with every bite.

Ingredients:

Pastry:
- 1/3 cup butter or shortening
- 1 ¼ cup flour
- ½ teaspoon salt
- 3 to 4 tablespoons cold water

Filling:
- 1 and 1/3 cup sugar
- 1 and 1/3 cup milk*
- 1 and 1/3 cup cream*
- 1 teaspoon cinnamon
- 6 egg yolks**

Instructions:

Pastry:

Step 1: Whisk salt into the flour.

Step 2: Cut the butter into small pieces and rub or cut it into the flour until the mixture has the consistency of sawdust.

Step 3: Add water one tablespoon at a time. Continue to mix until the dough is shaggy in appearance but can be rolled into a ball. Don't overwork the dough.

Step 4: Wrap the ball of dough in plastic, and chill at least two hours.

Filling:

Step 5: Preheat oven to 350°F. Roll out pastry and place in 9" pie pan at least 2" deep.

Step 6: Whisk the egg yolks, sugar and salt until smooth and glossy.

Step 7: Slowly beat in the milk and cinnamon.

Step 8: Pour the egg mixture into the pastry and bake one hour. Bake until it is set but still soft enough to quiver slightly when moved.

Step 9: When done, remove from the oven. Serve cold or warm.

* Instead of milk and cream, you can use 2 and 2/3 cups half and half.
** Peasants never wasted food. Use the egg whites for a fat-free omelette or other cooking.

Word search puzzle solution (see page 17).

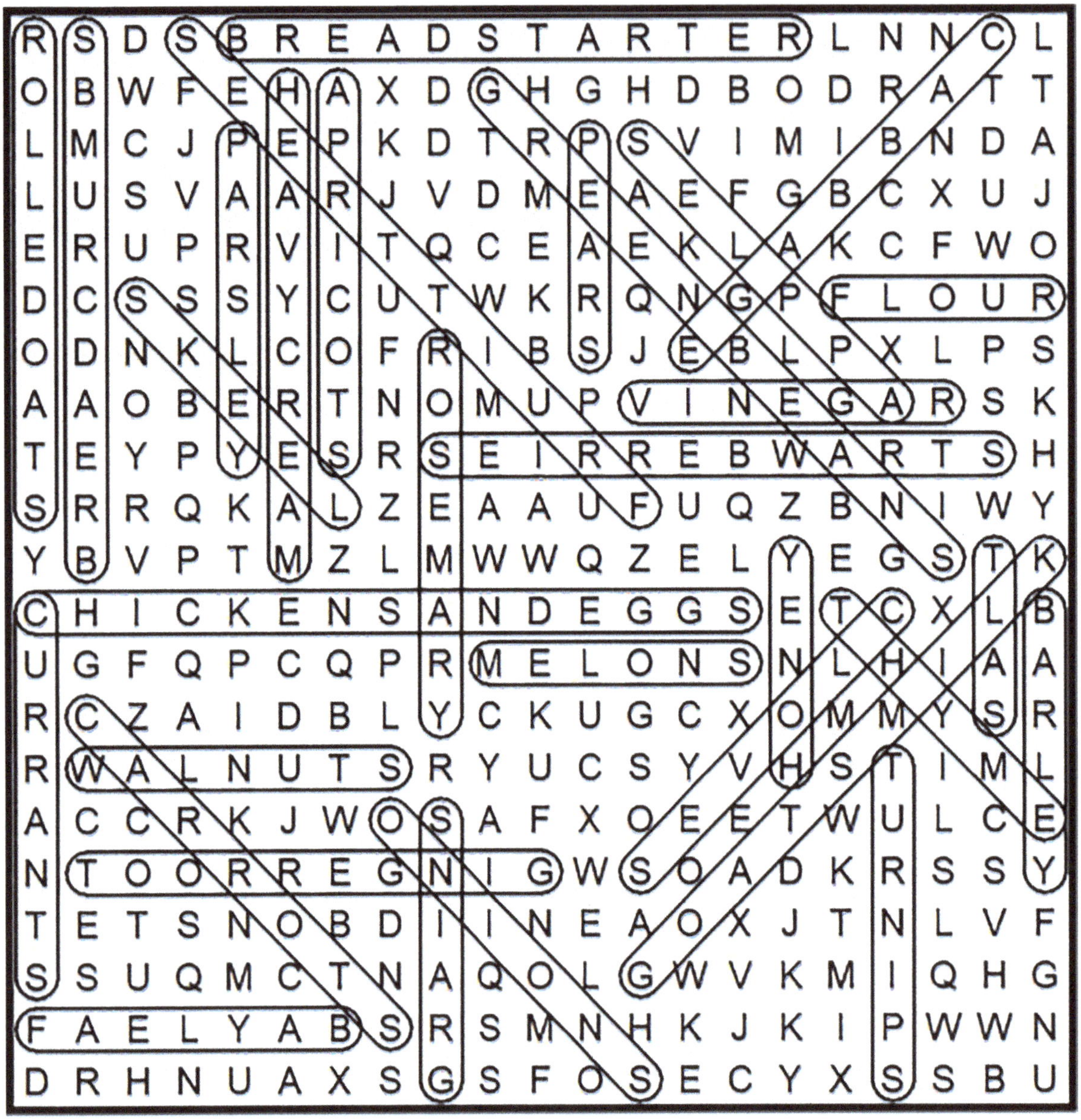

JACKSON
MARBLES

www.ingramcontent.com/pod-product-compliance
Lightning Source LLC
Chambersburg PA
CBHW061116070526
44583CB00027B/3315